BUCK FEVER

Deer Camp Cartoons

by Bruce Cochran

WILLOW CREEK PRESS

Minocqua, Wisconsin

For Bob and Carl

ISBN # 1-57223-001-0

Published by WILLOW CREEK PRESS
              an imprint of Outlook Publishing
              P.O. Box 881
              Minocqua, WI 54548

For information on other Willow Creek titles, write or call
1-800-850-WILD.

Printed in the U.S.A.

"What'll we watch next, gang? 'Field Dress Your Buck In Thirty Seconds' or 'Know Your Deer Sign'?"

"You don't mind if I take along my boom box and a few Grateful Dead tapes, do you Dad?"

"Try not to spill my bottle of coon pee on the meat loaf."

"If I studied my schoolwork as hard as you study those ballistics tables, I'd be a straight-A student."

"Wanna see a doe scent that really works? Watch this!"

"Six dozen eggs, ten pounds of bacon, four boxes of pancake mix . . That should get us through the first morning."

"Hope Mom doesn't get too lonesome while we're gone."

*"It's not like they didn't take you because they don't **like** you. They're going deer hunting."*

"I don't even care if I shoot a deer. I'm just going for the solitude."

"There must be some mistake. They gave me a 'Neither Sex' tag."

"The salesman said a five-year-old child could set this tent up. Go see if you can find one!"

"If we promise to enjoy nature all day, can we go into town and play video games tonight?"

"They've got both kinds of music out here: Country **and** Western."

"I've always said a boy can learn more on a trip like this than he could in school any day!"

"Is it just my imagination, or . . . ?"

"It's Bigfoot!" "It's a traveling junk heap!" "It's Uncle Charlie!"

"Chairs? Tables? What a bunch of wimps!"

"We have to remember not to bathe or use deodorant before we hunt. Uncle Charlie doesn't have that problem."

". . . So there he stood, biggest damn buck I've ever seen! Even bigger than the last dozen I told you about . . ."

"**Now** I remember what we forgot!"

"By the way . . . we brought a chainsaw."

"Mom never puts Wild Turkey in **her** chocolate cake."

"Who likes their steak burnt to a crisp and dropped in the dirt?"

"Wait till I tell the guys at school you wouldn't eat Dad's chili just because it had a little WD-40 in it."

"I thought you said we came out here to get away from women."

"It's either two big does and a buck, three small bucks, three big does, a doe with two big fawns, or three of the damndest fawns I've ever seen."

"Now we know where they're feeding."

"Somehow they seem to know the season doesn't open til tomorrow."

"It's called 'blaze orange,' and yes, you have to wear it even if you think it's dorky-looking."

"What makes you think you can concentrate on hunting while listening to a 'Twisted Sister' tape?"

"In this fog, we could be within ten feet of a buck and never know it."

"This muffler's still warm. I'd say Uncle Charlie drove by here about fifteen or twenty minutes ago."

"That's either one hell of a rub, or Uncle Charlie hit this tree with his jeep."

"They have an excellent sense of smell, but I'm not so sure about their eyesight."

"Lots of other hunters around, but no deer tracks."

"Try some of my trail mix, kid. It's made with chewing tobacco, deer liver, persimmons and squirrel nuts."

"I think I'm getting buck fever."

"One great thing about deer hunting . . . it gets you close to nature."

"We're not exactly lost. We just don't know where the hell we are."

"I've never seen him, but they say there's a monster buck that roams these woods. Rack this wide . . . probably weighs 300 pounds."

"You're sick, Roy. You know that, don't you?"

"I'm not sure I ever want to see this one."

"This is no ordinary deer we're dealing with."

"I figure they'll hole up in a warm, cozy place till this storm is over."

"They say an enormous buck lives in these woods, but I've never seen him."

"I've heard of Swiss Army knives and buck knives, but never a Swiss Army buck!"

"What do you figure this buck weighs . . . fifteen hundred, maybe two thousand pounds?"

*"I said the **old** logging road!"*

"I've always wondered how they kept track of all their rubs and scrapes."

"I figure they'll have to come here for water sooner or later."

"Missed! But I scared him!"

"That's the way it goes sometimes."

"I've never heard of 'Eggs A La Jack Daniels', but it doesn't sound bad."

"Who's ready for more pancakes?"

"You won't even know it's deer liver, kid. I flavored it up with some dog wormer."

"I don't know why everybody wants to eat in town tonight. I was planning on fixin' my famous 'Roadkill Chili'."

"Deer hunting means a lot to this little town."

"This looks like a good place."

"I'll have the 'Hunter Special' . . . without the powder solvent."

"I can't serve you kids the 'Hunter Special' til I see your Hunter Safety Cards."

"I ever tell you about the time I field-dressed a deer with a chainsaw?"

"Nobody shot him. He got into some of our coffee and just keeled over."

"Wonder how they made these french fries blaze orange?"

*"Are there any **deer** around here? Why Sonny, they come into town at high noon, walk right down Main Street, and pee on the school bus tires!"*

"Bang, bang."

"That reminds me . . . I forgot my hand warmer."

"I'll bet there's quite a story behind that."

"See you guys later. Gotta go in here and check my scrapes."

"You know that stocky little red-headed girl at the filling station, the one holding up the back end of the truck while they changed the tire? I think she likes you, kid!"

"Oh, my God! Hunters!"

"Last time I tore into one of these, all kinds of doo-hickies came flying out, and I never got it back together."

"With this full moon, they'll probably feed all night."

"Best damn doe scent on the market."

"Uncle Charlie says you have to think like a deer to be a good deer hunter."

"The way I look at it, four wheel drive just enables you to get stuck in a more remote area."

"How many times do I have to tell you? The **RED** lines are roads, the **BLUE** lines are rivers!"

"He was standing right here when I hit him. Then he jumped straight up in the air, and I never saw him again."

"I don't know about deer, but **I** can smell Uncle Charlie a hundred yards away."

"You don't suppose . . . . Naaaah."

"I estimated his range to be about 187 yards. Then, accounting for trajectory and bullet energy in foot-pounds, I shut my eyes and pulled the trigger!"

*"They're **plastic!**"*

"I saved the liver. At least **I think** it was the liver."

"I saved my deer liver to throw at girls at school."

"Looks like you could use a little help, kid."

"Wait 'til Boone and Crockett hears about **this**!"

"Kennel!"

"They'd help wildlife a lot more if they'd buy a hunting license."

"Want to go out for a hamburger after the protest?"

"Wanna talk about it?"

"We're looking forward to a shave and a hot shower . . . Uh, most of us, anyway."

"Eight-pointer . . . Shot him about seven this morning . . . Everything OK at home?
Any interesting mail? How're the kids?"

"My Hunter Safety Card? I traded it for an '80 George Brett and an '87 Kirby Puckett."

"You guys have got it backwards. You should make the **deer** wear blaze orange."

"All I like to do is hunt and fish. That's why I want to be a game warden."

*"The tag goes on the **deer's** leg, son."*

"You can have the hamburger dried and mixed with pipe tobacco if you want."

"Can you make my whole deer into one gigantic pizza?"

"Funny . . . It all fit before."

"Are you sure they didn't waste any?"

"Maybe we should have rented a trailer."

"Down a quarter of a tank! Looks like my turn to buy gas!"

"Hey, this is garbage! We must have put my dirty clothes in the dumpster!"

"Quick! Call a taxidermist!"

"If you find anything else of mine, burn it."

"How the Hell are ya, Mom? Wanna play some five-card stud?"

"Hi, honey!! How about a great big kiss?"

"Your laundry looks better in your jeans than you do."

"How about if I sit here and tell you how I shot my deer again while you wash all the dishes I brought home?"

"Scalpel"

"Save the giblets."

"Accent Redecorating? My husband is butchering a deer in the kitchen, and . . . "

"No venison quiche?"

"Can you make him look like he's got a bigger rack with more points?"

"Let's see a show of hands: Everyone who thinks this looks better over the mantle than
Aunt Wilma's painting of a grain elevator . . ."

"Do you realize there are only 350 days till deer season?"

Cartoonist Bruce Cochran brings his humor to us from a broad background in the outdoors as well as the arts.

Graduating from Oklahoma University with his Bachelor's in Design, he worked for Hallmark Cards as a writer/illustrator, and soon moved on to freelancing jobs with such publications as *Playboy, Look, The Saturday Evening Post, Sports Afield* and *Field & Stream.*

Cochran also has to his credit a daily sports section cartoon feature, "Fun 'N' Games with Cochran!" in the nation's #1 selling newspaper, *USA TODAY.* His children's book, *No Mind for Wellington,* first published in 1972 (Holt, Rinehart & Winston) is still in print today.

His interest in the outdoors makes him an avid hunter, fisherman and a collector of antique duck decoys. A sponsor member of Ducks Unlimited, his watercolors have been exhibited at the Easton, MD Waterfowl Festival and the National Ducks Unlimited Wildlife Art Show, among others.

Cochran is married to his wife of 32 years, has two children and has, he says, "been trained by a succession of three Labrador retrievers."